Beautiful Messenger

Gabrielle Jolie Malliett

authorHOUSE®

AuthorHouse™
1663 Liberty Drive
Bloomington, IN 47403
www.authorhouse.com
Phone: 1-800-839-8640

First published by AuthorHouse 8/13/2009

ISBN: 978-1-4490-0867-3 (sc)

Printed in the United States of America
Bloomington, Indiana

This book is printed on acid-free paper.

On January 17, 2006, Gabie was released from the hospital for the third time in a year, again from a drug overdose. The three of us (Clay, Gabie, and I) sat in our living room, Gabie plucking away on her MySpace, and Clay and I begging her to "please call this number; we can go there and just check it out." We wanted her to accept help for her drug addiction and enter a program. I really believed that one day she would outgrow her addiction with a little help.

Her response was the same as always: "I don't have a problem." How do you convince someone that she has a problem when she doesn't see it? I gave up and walked away. It was like talking to a brick wall. I didn't try hard enough, something I will live with forever.

Maybe she didn't see her drug addiction, but how could the hospital have not seen it? Every time Gabie was admitted to a hospital, it was to the same hospital and always with the same prognosis, a drug overdose. Why didn't they commit her? Do what I could not? After all, they had her trapped with the possibilities to help her, isn't that why they are there, to help the sick? Was it the lack of insurance or the attitude of her just being another teen with a drug problem, or was it that they wanted her out of their facility so a bed would be opened for someone more deserving? This time on January 17th they released her to someone who supplied her with the very reason she was there, drugs, just two hours after they had put her on a twenty-four-hour watch.

January 30, 2006, for the second day in a row my dinner consisted of my comfort food, oatmeal, a food I typically ate when sick. Yet for some reason I felt like I needed its comfort on January 30 and again on

January 31. I ran home from my primary job to eat and head off to my second job. It looked like Gabie had just gotten out of bed; nothing was picked up around the house. I had very few good things to say to her. One I remember clearly was, "You're a drug addict!"

Her response was, "If you think I am, I might as well be one!" I didn't hug her or tell her I loved her; I just watched her walk out and slam the door.

In less than twenty-four hours, I was told that I would never see my daughter again. My last words to her were truthful and honest, too truthful and honest for my memory. Words I believed she would see as truth one day and stop her addiction. Maybe then we could begin to have a wonderful life. I would become the mother I wanted to be, she the daughter with a future. But it never happened. Within a few hours, Gabie quit breathing. This time no one would call 911; she would sleep forever. Another drug addict passed from this earth. The hospitals would have one more open bed.

The doctor who performed the autopsy informed me that she could have been saved if only someone had called 911 in time, just like so many times in the past. But this time in the place she lay, the other inhabitant was off shopping, believing she was sleeping instead of struggling for her life.

Eighteen days after Gabie died, February 18, 2006, around 10:00 AM it was lightly snowing, a snow I typically would have enjoyed, reminiscing of when my children built a snowman or flapped their arms and legs against the ground to form that perfect angel. The flakes came down in light bellows; it was beautiful despite its disappearing act as it hit the ground. On that particular February 18, I barely acknowledged its presence, despite it being the only real snow of the season. I was on a mission and didn't have time to look out the window and remember; besides, remembering hurt too much. As I look back, I was always on a mission during those early these days, a mission to find anything that might give me an insight as to why I hurt beyond words. That day I

2

wanted to find a ring I had made for Gabie's eighteenth birthday. In the past when Gabie was careless with her things, I would pick them up and put them in a safe place for the future, when she might take better care of it. The reasonable place for me to have put it would have been in my jewelry box. I opened one of the three small drawers, the ring was not there, but a folded piece of paper was. As I unfolded the paper, I discovered a masterpiece I could not remember viewing prior to February 18, I truly believe this message was a gift from Gabie. Since that day, I have framed her gift to me and still wonder how it was delivered, where it came from, and what it meant. I guess I ask too many questions and should just accept her gift of the following picture on a snowy day: "I love snow."

I have always been skeptical of those who tell of similar experiences. I believed that the tellers' stories were just illusions of things they wanted so badly that somehow their minds created the impossible. Today I question some of my own experiences, could they be my brain and heart playing tricks on me, or are they real? One thing is for sure: the following writings from Gabie are real. Many have told me they are gifts to me from her. I believe they are gifts that hurt beyond her words and the lack of mine to save her. I am learning to accept her gifts despite the hurt they bring me. I now believe the dead communicate with those left behind I need to believe this.

About a month before Gabie died, I asked her if she had her writings in a safe place. She asked me why, and I explained that I had always enjoyed reading her stories. I now share them with you. I hope you too will enjoy her tales. Some are dark, others silly. Remember as you read that they come from a sensitive sixteen to seventeen-year-old. Many of Gabie's feelings are typical of her age Some come from pain, want of love, and some from a drug-induced state. Some are fictitious; others were very real. Before she died, I was privy to only a few of her tales and poems. Some I believe would have been eye-openers to a blind mother, if I could only have seen.

to:
my
MOM
and I love snow.
my
dad for: Gabe.

MAY 23, 2000

As I walk alone ... with you ...
I feel the need to run and grab your hand into mine
and hold on for dear life.

Your hand melts into mine,
as your body did,
and as it melts it sinks deeper into bliss,
intangible.

The beauty of the experiences shared is unspoken,
always cherished and never forgotten
just to be happy for that one moment is beauty
only we may share, together.

Each time I melt with you it's different;
the enjoyment soars
if only for a brief moment.

I know none of you will ever look into my eyes,
hold my melting hand and feel the same
but the oncoming traffic in your mind grows
prospers to a new beginning.

You truly are a good friend
and in some way
I will forever love you...

I just wonder what you see when you look at me.

I hope it's something great,
nothing branded with an evil smile.

I could never live with myself if I hurt you in any way...
You truly make me want you
thank you
forgiving a piece of you to me...

May 24, 2000

The emptiness I have surrounds me.
it seems as though it's all I have left.

I realize now there's nothing I can do,
but sit here and wait…
for what,
something great?

No, nothing will ever come.
I do not dare go to it and find it myself
for I have been lost for quite some time now
and will never find myself out of this hugh hole I have made.

I would love and I anticipate the need
to let go of the horrible things that come out of my mind and yours,
but I feel as though I'm unforgiving
and dare not look into your eyes to find the tears I gave you.

I think you're ******
I was your toy,
the one you played with and pretended to come for.

I am so empty…
though every now and again I become filled,
it's not as great as when you first began.

I hate this retribution I seek
I feel the need to find tranquility in my heart

and mind that's in love with misanthropies,
the only real thing that speaks to me.

I need and feel empty
the beauty in my writing is gone;
it's lost, and no more will come of it.

This may as well be the last of the things I write
the beauty is gone and I feel empty
so now I will wait and begin to weave a new beginning
from the things that will never be so great.

May 25, 2000

୫ଚ

My guilty pleasures are meaningless…
they take my body over and control my mind.

Who have I become, what have I grown into?
I keep asking and begging for more
why can't I see it doesn't work?

Why do I keep saying yes
to something so vile and horrible
what have I become?

I try to straighten up, and I try to say no… no more,
but the words never leave my mind
they just become analyzed and contemplated.

The more I give in
the more I grow to a being unlike my own
so far from reality.

The feelings that grow inside are realized by a feeling of pleasure
I can't seem to care about it
nor stop myself.

Who do I belong to?
What has become of me?
the emptiness in me has made me lazy and hateful.

I do not,

ever again wish to look in the mirror at myself
and the people I've grown to hate for my own faults.

I've got these pretty jitters, you know
the ones you can't shake
I do believe, however, it's because last night I was so baked…
now my jitters won't leave,
and all I do is wait for them to hide up my sleeve.

God, I hope they stay
the feelings of them are so great,
I feel as though I will never again hate
the things of annoyance from a past love mate.

I should now begin and seek out the buoyancies in my life,
find my very own knife
yes, that's it,
the knife I will use to cut open your spleen
and sell it to the jitters on my cloudless, mindless lake of emotions.

emotions.

Why do you ask if my keen sense is jitter fixed?
I don't know this, nor why they won't say good-bye
I will just anticipate the arrival of falling down on a hard path
the things that hit my mind
could never make me laugh.

I will always remember those justified and jitterfied days,
the ones that made me think
and anticipate the sight of the beautiful, long ocean bays.

Blunt to my hips,
Pocket full of chips;

When there's a cure
for pain, that's when I'll
put my drugs away

—morphine
(underground
Detroit jazz)

May 26, 2000

Whenever things start to make a little bit of sense,
I usually somehow screw them up
once again...

You came to me,
you found me out,
and I gave you that stupid piece of paper that spoke my mind
as when you screamed yours.

But my paper is hurtful and mean,
you were going to try and make things better;
even if you didn't see it
you were going to.

But now since I gave this white slip of dread and hate,
I wonder what you'll do...
will you run,
will you cry,
will you scream?

Whatever it is, I'm ready for it,
for I feel numb and old
and don't care what's going to happen to me
in my mind....

I don't care or anticipate what you'll do next
I don't know why I don't care
I don't know why I feel numb and helpless to you...

But I'm not really helpless
I just show no sign of emotion,
and in some way I'll always be motionless
I see that now...

Like the summers I spent as a child in my house
not outside,
not in the dirt and beauty of nature,
but in the ****ing doors of my four-walled prison
too emotionless to move...

These flashbacks of life fill my head with thoughts,
and somehow I realize I'm glad I gave you that white dreaded slip,
for when I get my flashbacks,
I've never once seen you in them...

That alone is what I like
to think of the fun times we had
I can't remember but know they were there
I can't remember 'cause I don't want to.

The closer I get to loving something,
the further I push it away,
but that's me,
and nothing anyone does will ever change that feat of life.

When I do think of your reaction
I think of the way you'll move your lips and eyes,
the way they will curve and form an assembly line of their own,
all demanding different functions to be done.

Maybe what you say is a trap
maybe it's a cry for help
whatever it is, I'm numb,
so I will walk on…

For I've been beaten down enough and don't want it from you
You give yourself away
by the way your personality changes in heartbeats,
so I will run and never again think about it.

That will be my cowardly way out
but the very best I can think of.
So now you deal with it
I just want to be left alone

but only for a while…

MAY 29, 2000

Oh God, it's beautiful.
I can smell the air and feel the sandy, sharp wind.
The voices in my mind
seep to the shore on the blue waves...
the people around me are kind and only see the outside of me.

It feels good to be away.
Nature is so warming to my heart
the beach smiles to me as I walk along,
and my mind drifts with the waves...
forgetting the hurt that was leading me to it.

Peace is coming in a big ship;
I just haven't seen it yet
I'll wait here forever
and look for the big white sail alone,
something blue.

I will stand at the edge of the ocean
and know somewhere, someone's standing there with me.
I will think of ways to fill my belly and mind
in order to have a good night's rest with you.

The beauty of this place surrounds me,
takes over my mind and soul.
I can't wait to go home...

June 8, 2000

Have you ever stared at something so long…
it no longer made any sense to you
really
me either…

I don't think I've ever really thought about anything that long
I guess I have no patience,
or maybe it's just in my nature to pass the little things away…
you know.

Of course you wouldn't…
you've got no mind
what the hell!!!
you talk of stupid things!

Like I'm dumb
'cause I talk of staring at things for too long…
you're dumb;
you don't stare at things at all and see them for not what they
are
but who they are.

The colors have never taken you over
and sheltered you from the white cloud of rain
*you're the ****ing dumb one,*
no, not me.

You're absentminded,

you listen to songs and don't hear a damn thing
no drums, no words, no guitar, no nothing
you're dumb and silent to the world
you're dead...

I'm gonna go on living and be queer
okay, hold on...
wait a minute ...
just let me ask you,
why,
why do you do this to yourself?

Are you afraid?
Well me too,
but I can still live with my eyes open,
or at least try.

What's your excuse?
Really?
that's not good enough.

I didn't mean it
you're not really dumb
I'm sorry!
tell me why, please...

you're afraid,
okay,
so we've already talked about that...
Ohh...
you're afraid to love??

Love, what, nature?
Well just look
open up your eyes,
take off your clothes;
they shelter you from too much,

Come… don't be afraid,
just do it
Wow! See,
isn't it great???

Now walk barefoot and naked,
free… run… jump…
play in the dirt,
swing on my branches
listen…
Hear it?
Hear the peace.

Aren't you glad you've meet me?
Me too
I love you,
you're so beautiful…
Good-bye, friend
I will meet up with you soon.

June 20, 2000

A thought:

Did you know that you live in an ugly hell
yup... you do
you live in a hell full of people who want to kill
and rape the nature of the world.

The now-ugly world,
the place where you must step around the edges of life
to find your own way and then, that will never be enough
nope, you're screwed
but we all are in some way or another.

I hate it here,
but I could never break free,
my dreams are consumed
with the little girl inside me.

Do you remember the time when my cat killed a mouse
and left it alone on my ugly concrete driveway
it just lay there,
not to be eaten but hunted for sport.

Feeling bad for this ugly creature,
which had never been seen as ugly or dirty in my young eyes,
I picked it up and carried it to my mother and father's bathroom,
where I proceeded to give it cough medicine.
It didn't work.

My mother came into the room screaming at me
I did this many times later, and when it wouldn't work, I'd just cry
not understanding why the mouse had to die
it was in one piece.

And why did my mother yell and take me to the doctor?
I just wanted to help the animal
I just cried being confused
it's scary not understanding the things you wish you could.

I guess I get the meaning now:
my cat is evil like the future I belong to
my mother is a society of screaming people trying to improve it ,
the animals stay dirty and untouched by superior hands
the cough medicine must be the healing power that wants to work but will
never work because it's not made for animals only humans.

I think now that I was trying to help but not quite making it
at least I never gave up
in the beginning I felt for the poor, helpless
creature.

I don't understand
the meaning of the world
and therefore never stood by it.

Whatever you do, it's not enough,
not until you keep on ..
doing forever and ever,
and ever then it's not enough.

Gabie was about six years old when I walked into the bathroom where she was wrapping a Band-aid around a mouse's neck as it flopped back and forth. Yes, my first reaction was to scream; it was also a moment that my daughter melted my heart, for hers was larger than mine for such a small creature. I did take her to a doctor a few days later, but not because of the love she felt for the mouse, but because the mouse had shared its lice with Gabie and in turn the rest of the family.

She was too sensitive for this world. Where many of us develop a mechanism to shut out the hurt, Gabie's emotions stood wide open.

June 21, 2000

A good friend came over the other day,
when I was feeling miserable about myself.
He asked,
"Do you know the new Third Eye Blind CD?"
and I'm like, "Yeah, why?"
He explained that a song on it is like him singing to me.

I listen,
and think about the song and cry even harder than I am already
no one will ever know me like Daniel
or ever see me the way he does.

I change around him to the real me,
and I become built into him
in a way he was singing the song to me,

he wrote it in my mind
for me.
I love you, Daniel!!!!!

WOUNDED.

My Song:

Why can't you see?
Any of you,
why can't you be?

What's the matter with the feelings I have,
why can't I believe in what you ask,
my new ideas,
my new feelings?

Why don't you believe me when I say my mind?
You're so blind,
you can't believe a damn thing,
why, why?
Please, believe me...
please...

I'd love to have a new person
to reach out to me,
grab my bags
let's go, you'd say.

But why,
why?
Please, believe me,
please.

July 11, 2000

જી

How do you feel on top of a great pyramid of scenes and seederals?
What do you see yourself doing in the near future:
artist, lawyer, teacher,
perhaps someone who will make a difference,
a meaning of truth and self-righteousness,
a lover???

Could you be all those things?
Is it your time to be hesitant?
Are you a Morrison,
believe in divine righteousness...
what's your gift in an empty world?
Will it help?

Can you knock down your wall of conformity and righteousness,
could it be you're a survivor?
Do you see and love
wherever you're headed
in the directions of the gods themselves or your own?

Getting back to nature is pure, simple bliss
are you bliss-less
do you feel?
I'll feel for you,
love you,
cherish you...

Come back to me and love me as yourself,

as nature loves.
Come back to nature
it belongs to no one,
but longs to hold and grasp you
try to hold and grasp
feel it?

July 13, 2000

A late-night thought…
maybe mystery!

Where do I lie,
in a bed covered with staining
sinking satin?

Beauty
comes to my lips
it drinks me and supports my evil deeds to trust and understanding.

My love lies in the ocean of pure blue mistless moss,
waiting and wanting to understand a loveless life,
contemporary in peace and thought.

My spiritual self must remain concise,
learn to spell the words of life,
hear my echoes of gifts and findings.

Believe in me
as I believe in you
of all being you're my one shining star.

The beauty in your glory on each and every day
never be overlooked
by the beings of day-to-day life.

The loveless ones see and hear you call to them for the love in you

ask me questions, and I'll do my best to answer
the pity in your life and charm.

The beginnings in your mind never end
the strife to remain in a safety of walls and coverings on the books,
word unspoken to life.

Your beauty ends in a simpler world of magic??

July 14, 2000

To let the daylight in
is a big risk on beginning a new journey
to let the emotions and truth show
is a big waste of resources on your part.

To give a shit about any of it
is a timely, costly problem you must solve.

To not solve it
would be an unjustice of many kinds
the guidance
 in the scripture of your life has been diminished.

Withered and dried out,
laid down to rest.

Let the light shine in through your eyes of darkness
the random times will take you over
and captivate your soul.

To you...

Somewhere in time

꙰

Who is this person before me?
Look,
look you will see her...
look,
I don't think she's pretty;
she's so plain, and I don't like the person she's become.

Yes, you're right
I'm right, she makes me sick
I do believe she's lost something great in her,
but what?
can you see it from here?

Can I?
can you help her
what?
Help?
Oh yeah, help her find what she's lost...

No,
no, I can't,
I mean you can't; she's too far gone for us,
me to reach...
She's so ugly now,
I'm.

I mean she's shriveled up and dried out
yes, laid down to rest, but I,

she does try
(I do?) she does,
she tries what?

To be something she's not
yep, she will no longer enjoy
myself,
herself, ever…

Why do you believe
I'm, she's like this?
Who knows, we don't
she doesn't, I mean
look, look at her now, she's doing something…
look.

Yes, I am, I mean, yes she is,
she's crying….
emotions pour from her soul
will anyone listen to me?
To her.

Nope, no one around me,
I mean her at this moment in time
my handwriting's become sloppy;
hers has become sloppy
I wonder why?

Can't you see she's sorry
for what (what am I sorry for?),
for all the wrong I have done,
she has done?

And through it the star dripped down and melted
and now all that's left is a tiny, ugly, plain girl
with the scars of a river and tears that so often flow through it.

Embrace It

God, I know that I screwed up,
that I screw up!
I'm sorry;
I don't know how to keep on the right path and defeat my own demons.

Please don't forget about me,
Please don't stop loving me
I mean well,
I try to do well.

Please show me the right path
Please help me achieve his love
I want to forget the other one
and achieve his love.

With time I can help him and his addictions
unless I'm one of them
and then I will embrace it

Please help.

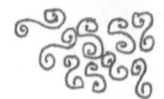

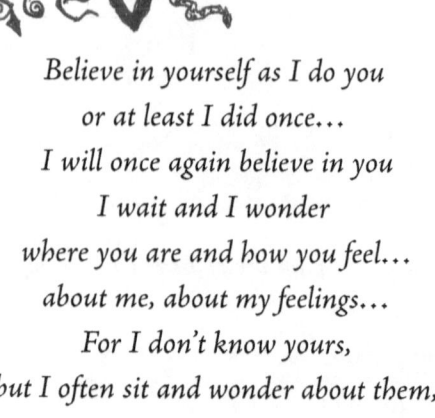

Believe in yourself as I do you
or at least I did once...
I will once again believe in you
I wait and I wonder
where you are and how you feel...
about me, about my feelings...
For I don't know yours,
but I often sit and wonder about them,
yes I do,
I often sit right here and
wonder about what you see
when you look around,
when you look at me.
Into my eyes...
I think of how wonderful it would be to meet you
and walk with you in your beautiful eyes.
The plainness of your smile could somehow show me the way...
I miss you and your touch,
the beauty of your hands
once healed me and I loved it.
For as of now
I need healing,
I need your sweet touch
within all my selfishness I need you...
Please touch me once more...
I believe you can.
Why, does your beauty blind you
from all the things you're supposed to see???

Untitled

Untitled
unsaid…
unspoken…
something so unexplainable
something so great…

Your emotions soar
and your heartaches…
do you know what it is???

It is something so beautiful,
something great and unknown
how do you feel this moment?

I myself am sitting here
writing this to you and feeling so strong,
so great.

Do you still not know what it is?
How do you feel while you're reading this?
What is going through your beautiful mind… head, body?

I feel the rush of something great
the feeling you can never shake once it's started
do you understand what it is?

Do you believe in yourself,
do you have your goals obtained

or are you confused
laid down to rest?

Peace is within you
you will find it some way or another
I have,
I know how I feel...

happy...
happy...
the joy in my heart...
happy...

Whoever

Dear whoever you have become
I write this to you,
as my thoughts flow
I can't believe I'm doing it.

My thoughts flow right off this paper
and onto a dream
I've dreamt it so many times.

Oh God I hate it when it storms
maybe if you were real
you'd make this loud anger stop…

But you're not real
and probably never were
so for now you can't do a damn thing to make it stop.

You're shit,
you're nothing to these people you preach about helping
I myself am amazed they want to believe in you.

Maybe they're just weak and need something to hold onto
you give no mercy and don't help anyone why?
Why do you hate me so much?

It's not in any way my fault your world is hell.
can't you just do me this one favor and make it stop,
this noise is killing my ears.

Why do you feel the need to punish me so?

But yes,
I'll admit it's a beauty and marvel to see,
but Goddamn it, it's so loud.

Don't you care?
Will you just sit there on your high pedestal and look down upon your
*****ing empty world,*
a world that doesn't believe in you.

For you have shamed us all
is that what you'll do
glance down on me?

For you're not real and will never be real in my eyes
you don't help,
you can't make this loudness stop.

You're useless
I'm so sorry you had to find it out this way
I will never forget you, but I can try.

I will bring you up in my conversations,
*analyze the **** out of you,*
just as you do me
on my so-called judgment day.

I'll laugh right in your face…
and then get down on my grazed knees and cry
this will continue for hours,
for I do not know why but I will.

Maybe I don't want to not believe in you
and then be punished severely for it.
I just don't know.

So I write this to you and ask you
who, who do I look to,
turn to,
to answer each and every one of my questions?

Please, help me
thank you
sincerely,
me,
a browned-haired short girl
in an empty world.

I Wish I Could Just Help You Find
an Easier Way Out of Your Troubles

Mr. Magoo loves him
He's beautiful
in his own extra-special way
Only I can see him standing alone.

He cries, but no one answers him
No one person can see his pain…
He covers it with a thick, wet blanket of wool.

The wetness is from the drool he sprays
to the millions of people in his dreams
that every so often become reality.

He tries to hide his pain in a storm of guilt he saves for everyone else;
he tries to make them feel bad for the things they have done or stand for,
but only in order to make sure they never see his faults…

When something comes too close to him,
he pushes it away with all his might
even though it hurts him to do this,
he never shows it in the front.

But we all know that when he is alone,
he is consumed with his thoughts and lies
he tries to make the voices stop dead in their tracks,
but they don't listen;

they have taken over his soul,
his sweet, innocent soul.

No matter what he does, I will love him
He cannot push me away so easily
I'll come back and help him fight…
if he'll just let me…

Sometimes I wonder…
I wonder where,
where I'm going, and with whom.
I sit down on my floor and think long and hard about things in my head
I hear people in my mind telling me what to do
I don't listen to them.

They're mean and cruel
they say I see only what I want to,
and I only hear the things that make me believe.

I still don't believe them
should I?
Should I let them control my life,
my destiny?
I don't know…

For now all I can do is sit here on my floor and feel lonely
it scares me;
the people around me scare me
what are they thinking when they say,
"Look into my deep blue eyes?"

I can only wonder and think about it,

for I do not know....
Where should I ask someone about it?

Would that chosen person listen to me,
would they care or just push me away,
like every other person I come in contact with?

Why am I asking you?
What do you know?
You never helped me with a damn thing.

But I suppose if I don't ask you, I can't ask anyone,
so for now I'll just sit here
wonder, think, and wonder...
that will be my new quest.

To unravel the eerie things of the ones that you and I belong to,
who knows...
maybe I can make those mean and cruel people leave.

LIFE

Life:
what is the meaning of something so insignificant…

To grow old,
to grow happy,
to grow sad,
to grow…to die…
why, what is the cause…?

Does anyone know the answer to the greatest mystery on this small
planet…,
do you?

That is what you once asked me…
and I looked at you with all your glory and slowly answered…,
no, I'm sorry, I don't know.

Then you turned around and cocked your head and cried
you sat there with your head in your hands and cried
I must have seen a thousand tears drop from your salty eyes…

I'm so sorry that I did not run after you,
save you from your tears
can you please forgive me???

For now I will never forgive myself for the pain I caused you
you truly are the reason
as to why I stay here on this small, lonely planet of ours…

To Forgive...

᎐

To forgive:
I want to,
I feel I need to,
but I don't know how...
I will begin to try
with an unknown help
I will begin to heal these wounds and bruises you have given me...

As I sat there, lying on the ground looking up,
staring up into the early morning sky,
I wondered...
I wondered why,

why me out of all the beings on this great, insignificant planet...
why me...
why did you have to choose my body to bruise and flounder about your
own...?

Do my tears mean anything to you?
You took my body and tore it into a thousand pieces with your big ugly
hand;
you took my mind and sold my soul..

I will never forgive you
for what you have done to an innocent,
but for now I will forget all about you and your evil ways.

I shall focus on myself and anger I have to bring you out...

I think now why,
why did I leave the security of my mother's bed to go into yours.

I did not mean to run into you;
it just happened you found me...

I wish I could have known you,
then maybe...
understand what you've done to me...

I first need to forgive myself
for my faults,
then maybe I can work on yours...

Maybe I knew you,
but I guess I do in some way
you're a man, a sad, obviously lonely man...

I feel bad for the people you've hurt and the ones to come
you are the most insincere son of a bitch I know,
and I feel for the wounds you must have...

Please, please let me forgive you for your ways
I know now I will never see you again
and pray to the stars I look at now that I don't.

I don't hate you
but shall never find a damn thing to like in you,
do you really believe I deserved to be dead to the oncoming world and numb
in their eyes???
So now as my story continues...
I will get up and go to my mother's unprotected shelter of life and love.

I will walk a thousand miles and still never forget you,
but to forgive you, I shall use up my time and bite my lip...
to become normal once again
I stand and wonder how your story continues to end...

When Gabie was 16, a junior in high school, she went to her school counselor and told her she was raped. The counselor and I spoke several times about the issue, and I explained that Gabie had recently told me the same story. I asked Gabie how she wanted to handle it—find this person and prosecute him? Gabie told me that it had happened two weeks earlier, and it was too late. It was on one of the many nights she had sneaked out of the house, and it had occurred in our neighborhood not far from our home. Gabie did not want to find this person and refused to file any type of police report. I often doubted her accusations, as did the school counselor. We felt something happened but doubted that Gabie was telling us the whole story or maybe even the truth. I did take her to a professional psychologist so she could talk to someone. But little came out of these visits, although we continued them for several years. After January 31, 2006, when I found her journals and read the above I again questioned the incident. After reading her words in "To Forgive," I only doubted my reactions as a mom. How could I doubt her, why didn't I know, maybe sense the truth in her statement? All I could do was once again chalk it up to being a horrible mother to my one and only daughter. As the nightmare of the first year of her death came to an end, I learned to forgive myself for some of my actions. To this day I am trying to remind myself that I loved Gabie immensely, despite many of my actions. I did not always doubt her, but as time progressed and Gabie's bipolar condition intensified, our day-to-day dealings with each other also intensified, and our trust in each other was many times lost. Some days it was hard to tell who was closer to a mental breakdown, Gabie or me from viewing her careless, dangerous behavior or the ranting and raving we both exhibited.

The beliefs of one to another
come to you in great and many times, ways, functions.
Believing is seeing
the beauty in life,
of not being ignorant to the world of surroundings and ideas.

My beliefs function solely on my mind and train of thought,
in being one with my spiritual undormant self,
the self I have newly found
but every so often I lose my grasp.

The spirits in me sing to the higher power of the so-called heavens above,
to not knowing or understanding the function of life come on to one.
I believe in myself
but don't understand or can't decide on what I am.

Who am I?
It frustrates and irritates my senses.
My ignorant bliss is gone, and my mind is fragile
tell me something that sounds decent, and I shall believe it,
mold into my body and tempt my soul.

Who am I to be
now that I justify all my words and morals and can gently break the ground
on which I stand?
I will never be true or as whole to myself
I can't keep this up forever.

July 20, 2000

What do you see when you look at me?
To be honest, I don't see shit
I see someone weak and fragile,
someone dead,
the untouched, full of a ghost.

I see someone who is no longer free to do as they please,
a person with baggage that no one wants to open.
The girl inside is molded to fit everyone's needs,
your needs, not hers
she exists only for your pleasure
because you allow her to.

Should you help her?
No, watch her die
please feel free to help in the process,
push her
you know she's weak
because of you and words and deeds you've done to her.

Go ahead and rape her insides,
tear her into pieces to nothing,
rape her life and heart.

There is no sewing you can do to heal her wounds
it's too late for all of that.

Just look at her, no longer pretty;
tears fill the gaps and holes in her life

she breathes when you tell her to,
even though you know in your heart she means nothing to you,
yet you still keep her

Why?
For laughs,
kicks,
or to push her around and kill her slowly with words.

Her opinion is nothing
and all that she stands for is shit to you,
you've killed an innocent girl
by the tongue in your mouth.

When she was a child,
she was happy and free
you were her reason to live, her everything
what you have done to me deep inside I hope you will never know.

I think, you think I'm stupid
you think I don't understand
she's lost her name now.

I have lost my name now;
I'll never find a new one
she is perfect in that ****ed way.

She looks like she used to be happy with the girl inside
she is the saddest girl I've ever known
she wakes up in the middle of night just to say everything will be all right

I think she could have been happy in a better life.

I'm crying for you

Just in case you're wondering
I wrote this while I was tripping…
I know, stupid…
right???

Well this is how I felt…,
so bear with it.
The night I wrote this, I will never forget…
due to the events that later came…

Are not we all dead in some form or another?
I can't stand it…
this being alone
I can't stand bearing it…

Death the only thing that will ever speak to me…
I need…
I want to die…
to be alone.

I keep waiting and holding on to something—
what???
Something now so wonderful… hopeful
I need that little dose of reality,
reality that's touched my life.

I need you, your touch… your life,
you of one being of all great things…
I need you
please help me… reach a goal in my life.

Can't you see…
I'm dying,
I'm crying for you
Love me,
please me, touch me…

I'm crying for you
I can't do this anymore
please belong to me
I miss something in my life that made it…

TO YOU

You let me in your life,
and by doing so you've touched me in your very own beautiful way
I wish I could thank you for the warmth
you've given me,
but I do not know how.

The many nights we've spent together
in deeply blue grass
don't mean anything to you in a practical sense.

You listen to me and hear my words,
but your face is empty and solemn
you seem alone.

I hope you keep me for a long time
I truly want to hold and comfort you in your darkest hour,
let me...
let me love and hold you in my strong arms
if I do, will you return the favor?

Will you love me back,
cherish me in some way, fashion, or form?
I feel the need to be with you,

as what I don't know:
friend,
lover.

For now I'm content with the friendship you've bestowed upon me
within that I see your love.
I look on to the late-night hour and dream of our talks
of life and cultural disbeliefs
I truly hope the words you speak of, and seem to believe in, are real.

No Comments Please, thank you
(unless you really think I need one)

Oh my God,
its 10:10 PM,
and I'm sitting on my floor staring at the damn phone.
What's wrong with me,
why do I get this way?

I feel so alone
I know I'm not,
but I just feel alone
like no one really cares about who I am and what I do.

The first day of school, and depression and insecurity fills my surrounding
air
it's sick really
that I feel alone
am I that vain???

But then maybe I'm right,
all of my friends seem to be not real, they're distant.
Why do they really keep me around?
I wonder why
what good am I to these people?

I guess I just want to feel alive,
but that got me into so much trouble before

you see for me to feel alive, means leaving my safety net;
that means sneaking out,
which is fun, but the consequences of my actions get me into lots of trouble.

I used to look to drugs to solve the loneliness,
but that got boring,
so now I'm back again to being happily sober
but at the same time frustrated and weak.

People let me down too much
I'm so afraid to leave and not wait for something,
someone...
Maybe I should talk to someone
I don't know
I think I need to paint.

Art is the way to life

Ahhhh!!!! It's so frustrating
I've never gotten a top locker,
and when it finally comes down to it, I get one,
but no...
because some idiot decides it would be better to put their own lock on it,
so I get moved to another top locker.
Guess what, someone else was there,
so now I get the bottom
that's my life,
I guess,
anyways, I'm almost always on the bottom
oh well, I can't change my luck
I'm not unhappy either,
so who cares?
I don't,
but I do
contradicting myself
comes so easy to me
why, I don't know;
it's really funny though....

August 9, 2000

Who am I really,
behind all my glitter
and words of wisdom.

August 10 Updated

I secretly switched mine with another top locker
Shhh!!
Don't tell.

Hypocrite

When I think I've got things straightened out,
I somehow manage to screw them up
why, I don't know;
it's just crazy.

My spirit is so tired but so restless
I want to be a good child,
but I can't
I'm not a bad daughter,
just a bad child.

Maybe I create drama in my life for the hell of it
and just haven't realized it yet.

I lost a piece of myself last night
when I left my home against my mother's wishes
I didn't even have a great time,
but I felt alive???

I've never wanted to take back the things I've done and said,
no matter how bad or good or mean (etc.) they were
'cause I live my life to the fullest, and if I died tomorrow, my soul would go
easily
'cause I live each day as if there's no tomorrow.

I want to be free from things,
but I hold myself back,
which I know is for the good of me.

I love my mother, and I hate hurting her for no reason,
but I do—why??
What's wrong with me?
I think I've started to lie about too many small things.

Maybe this is strange,
maybe not
I don't know,
but it's getting old and boring now…

I keep asking myself why???
Internal conflicts suck!

I can honestly say that Gabrielle was not a bad child. I do not believe there is such a character. I do believe she made some bad choices, ones that we fought over constantly. But the true Gabie had a heart that towered over most. She cried over the smallest of conflicts, but this is not to say she followed the straight and narrow or my every wish; she didn't. Many nights and early mornings I sat on our front porch waiting for her to come home after finding her bedroom window open and her bed empty. Other nights when exasperated I would lock the window and wait for the inevitable: a ringing of the doorbell, an argument over what she thought she was doing, her months of grounding to come, and then sleep knowing she was safe for a few more days.

AUGUST 11, 2000

I don't think any of my other pages in this journal will compare to the first
page.
I just feel that the first of anything can never be compared to.

I am hoping for something great to happen tonight
maybe it won't,
but hopefully it will.

I want someone to notice my glory for who and what I am,
but I don't really know who or what I am
struggling with identity is tough.

Last night I reconciled with an old friend
I still can't get over it
I showed him the poem I wrote for him, and he loved it,

God, that makes me so happy,
you have no idea
I love it
I love him.

I'm glad I'm a friend again
my emptiness is very slowly going away
it's a great feeling.

August 13, 2000

I'm really awful
I know now the way I present myself is not the right way at times
I can't make everyone like me.
I wish I could, but I can't
I guess I will just take what I can get.

I can't be high off life forever
sometime I got to come down,
sometime...
I wish he liked me, for who I am;
I wish he knew who I am
he doesn't though;
he sees in the wrong light.

That's okay, I just got to take it as it comes
it sucks though,
but what can I do
nothing really,
so oh well...

Watching someone (you)
telling a story of love and companionship
for someone who is now dead was amazing.
I felt as if I was watching a story on TV
about a struggling life less ordinary.

I loved it
I felt saddened by the drama involved in it,
it was beautiful to imagine the story actually taking place,
like there is something to be learned in it all.

AUGUST 15, 2000

Gone Like the Wind

I'm overwhelmed with crap,
and the worst part is that it's only going to get worse
it sucks
I got all this crap, but I'm too lazy to start, work on, finish, or complete it.

I don't want to be here I don't want to work.
Please let me go home and sleep
I hate this school.

The people here are so ignorant
they only hear and see what they want to,
when they want to;
they go on stereotypes, not personal knowledge.

I need to break free of here,
but I have no way of doing so
that's what really sucks…

It's so frustrating
I'm so tired,
but I got all this work and shit to figure out.

I just want to sleep
I'm tired of looking at my room;
it's too ****ing messy.

I know I have bad language.
It's funny; everyone thinks I look innocent,
like I totally got that "little girl" thing down
but in reality I'm so evil,
and I love it.

My innocence is so far gone;
my self-esteem is too
that's bad
I like being "evil," but I feel I have nothing left to hold back.
No more secrets to give
and that sucks, 'cause I don't feel special anymore
but that's my fault, no one else's
oh well. I say too much...
who cares, I don't

I think I'm burnt out
I got to get it together, really bad....
No more ACID RAIN on you tonight.

AUGUST 16, 2000

Today's been nothing but fight after fight with my mom
I really hate her at times.

Why does she feel the need to have so much power over me?

She thinks I can't see straight through her act of drama,
but I can:
it's crystal clear.
She can be so dumb at times
I'm amazed she lasted this long,
we've lasted this long.

I really can't stand people at times
they make me sick,
why do people assume things?
They make assumptions and can't back them up.
Oh well,

I like all the drama though:
being scared and seeing who will stand up for you
is awesome,
it's fun,
I love it
but it's frustrating too.

Gossip really does make the world go round,
but I don't gossip…
so I'm not into the "thing."
I'm gonna play it by ear
why do they have to pin you into corners so you can't walk away? Dumb!!!

PENS AND COLORS ARE SO FREE!!

My journal has taken on a life of its own.
I draw, write, color, and contemplate in this thing.
Plus I also let others do things in here as well.
That okay???
Right???
I hope so because I wouldn't have it any other way
I'm gonna keep my journal forever and ever
till it's filled;
then I'll start another.
Every page is special and makes me happy!!!

People

Contemplating and constructing endless ideas of life and love,
the possibilities or meaning,
hope, in justification,
the words that sing in the midmorning coffee,
shops of people…
chosen words,
the chosen few…
people.

AUGUST 21, 2000

Today's pretty
it makes me happy how pretty the day is…
I look forward to the morning
                    OH HAPPY DAY!!!

August **30, 2000**

Oh my God
I so wish I had this journal throughout the past two weeks
so much has happened
and it's so emotional,
but you know me
I only look to the future
so that's all I'm gonna write about...
sorry...

Friends

I think I got a new friend!!!
It's so great!!!
I'm really unbelievably happy!
My day's going by so great!!!
These days make everything worthwhile
I love it
when things seem perfect…
it makes me smile.

August 31, 2000

Ahhhh!!! I don't want to do this...
please, just let me sleep...
please...
I'm so tired.
I don't know what to do to get what I need for the weekend.
Planning sucks!!
Ahhhhh!!!!

September 1, 2000

Some people are so nice,
so willing to help you if you're struggling
from this all confusion comes in.
Do I like him or him?
Hmmm, "I wonder which,"
and it really makes no difference
'cause in a few months it will all be over,
but I guess the joy I showed at that time is worthwhile
I hope it is anyways.

SEPTEMBER 2, 2000

I think pretty people make pretty things.

SEPTEMBER 3, 2000

I like to paint and draw
it makes me feel nice after I finish and look at it
I think pretty people also say and do pretty things.

But what are pretty people
how can you tell if you're pretty
I mean, aren't we all supposed to be pretty?
I wonder.

I'm considered pretty...
I think I'm beautiful
as well as everyone else
does that make me pretty?

SEPTEMBER 4, 2000

I feel completely artsy
I don't know why
but I feel the need to run and jump,
skip and play
be free!!!
Freeway

SEPTEMBER 5, 2000

I think that I need to let go
of the past, and focus on the future.

I feel the need to make the best decisions for myself
and feel beautiful.

I like feeling free and not under the hand of Mother Culture;
she's so evil!

Mother Culture tells all the wrong from right,
but it's never good enough.

Oh well, I mean you can't please everyone,
especially not Mother Culture.
I don't even want to try.

SEPTEMBER 6, 2000

I hope and pray they don't ask me out,
I hate turning people down
I wish I could make myself like them,
but I can't.

I just don't feel it,
it's so sad
'cause maybe I led them on
and maybe I didn't—who knows?

But if they do, I know what I'm going to do,
but I'll feel mean and cruel
I hate that.

SEPTEMBER 7, 2000

I don't feel well today
I think I'm gonna lie around in bed all day...
until I feel better
sleep is such bliss

SEPTEMBER 8, 200

Just Draw

       it's okay.

SEPTEMBER 9, 2000

Love is in the air

SEPTEMBER 10, 2000

I hope he likes me
I don't know how to act or feel about him.
What do I say?
What do I do?

I just want to hold and never let go of him
how can I show him the light?
I'm his for the taking
I cherish our friendship;
if I make a move,
I could burn something beautiful.

So, now where does that lead me
should I ask him how he feels
hint around it?

Or get to know and understand him better,
learn how he functions?
My heart and mind one together but so far apart;
what do I do
say, think???

My story to me
should I let it be undisclosed,
who knows
who do I ask for help?

I can't tell or show anyone the feelings inside me;

it's so difficult
I need to be free from insecurities
and say and do what's on my mind,
they may affect the outcome of futures to come.

Get over it, if need be
or move on with him
maybe I'm just infatuated with him;
it's really too early to tell.

I just know, for now he'd be right for me,
I think I would be for him
I can't force him though
I guess I'll wait and let him make the first move.

Of course there's no harm in helping him along the way,
just to get a little started
I hope I get my own way.

DREAMING OF LOVE

September 11, 2000

He doesn't like me, not like that,
not for now anyways
I won't wait for him.

If he comes around,
then he does
I really don't think I want him.

Besides if I got him, our friendship would be ruined
I love him as a personal friend,
not a boyfriend.

I'm just gonna move on,
forgive myself and forget him
under the circumstances we'd be together.

He tells me I'm a beauty,
model material;
he's a great friend.

I'm happy
with the choices he's made
he makes me think and admire him.

SEPTEMBER 12, 2000

I feel free, so happy

Freedom is essential to life,
I know now I can get up and do anything I want,
be any person
I feel as though I have no enemies, and people really like me.

It makes me happy when they say,
"you're unique," "different," "cool," etc.
I love it,
it's like as soon as I stopped caring about what people think,
that's when they started to see me for myself.

It's really ironic
but great
as long as I'm nice and kind to everyone and anyone,
I can do no wrong
I love people.

Everyone is equal in my eyes,
I used to dream of being those girls that everyone socialized with;
befriend the preps, blacks, dorks, hippies, etc.,
all shapes, colors, sizes
I love it!

Even though I don't really have many close friends,
I've got my good friends that I know care
and would bend over backward for me,

and that really counts as long as I'm happy, right???

True to myself!!
That's all that will ever count
is the truth in myself and life…

September 13, 2000

I feel good
I didn't do any of my homework,
but I feel nice and special
happy feelings are in my heart; they creep through my mind and bones,
captures and takes me over.

SEPTEMBER 14, 2000

I love you, Miss Maturity!!!
You're great;
your class makes me so happy
It's like I used to think that art was my only outlet,
but drama has helped me release
my newly found creativity,
enlightened me to be myself and someone
I love it.

SEPTEMBER 17, 2000

Today I feel enclosed
I'm not at peace with myself and others
I need to go to bed and wake up to a new beginning.

SEPTEMBER 18, 2000

I'm tired and ill...
Sleep calls and sings
its lovely voice to me.

September 19, 2000

Everything is peachy keen!!!...
THE CORE OF MY EXISTENCE
I am a person
with thoughts and feelings
as any other person.

My existence at this point in time is meaningless
soon when I'm older,
I will have meaning

But for now
I am here
with no reason or right.

SEPTEMBER 24, 2000

ℰ℮

Oh my goodness, some of the weirdest stuff happens to me...

I just don't know what to think of it anymore,
how should I act
or handle my surroundings and environment???

I just don't know what's going on,
maybe I'm out of control
or just having fun...???
I can't decide at this exact moment.

But I do know I will read this later and laugh at myself for being dumb
oh well, such is life
I don't know where to begin
ask me questions, and I can help?

I just wish I understood why people and society work the way it does,
why people use drugs,
disobey laws and rules,
why people strive to be more then anyone else,
to conform and succeed.

Why do people use? A funny question for a person who would eventually die from the very thing she questioned. The above was a conversation between Gabie and a good friend of hers, Randy. At the time Randy was abusing alcohol and drugs, so much so that he joined a support group close to our home. Several nights Gabie went with Randy to give him support. I wonder if she listened?

September 25, 2000

I feel the need to be a good person
I want to make things right and nice
so I can get a peace of reality back.

SEPTEMBER 26, 2000

HELP!

September 27, 2000

I got to make up my mind,
to solve my problems
I feel they're getting worse when neglected.
I can't fail my tasks
they're scaring me
what do I do, and where do I go?

September 28, 2000

I got so much on my mind,
so much to do,
so little time.

What is time really
it doesn't matter what time it is;
you're still gonna live.

It's just something to keep track of events during the day
oh well, just another thing to work,
it never stops working
when does time get a break?
I feel bad for time.

SEPTEMBER 29, 2000

Who do you really belong to?
You think I don't see you;
you're dumb...
I see past your shadow.

It's you, all you, not one part is true.
You're so weak
you turn and think I won't see,
but I do, the whole damn game.

Flashing lights,
loud sound,
"the crowd"; they don't hide you.

You stick out like a thorn
I see you for all that you are,
just be yourself,
that's all...

You can't hide at all
be free from conformity,
be yourself
for you do have it all...

The only thing I regret is nothing...

One of the best travel guides on the windy road of life is yourself...

Love who you are and cherish yourself!!

You've always had the power!!!

Bad things happen to good people
why do so many suffer
and become hated in eyes of hypocrites and sinners?
Actually we are all "sinners."

Who is to judge the courteous and good,
deemed by what right
who is perfect and kind?

Ask and you shall receive... what?
What goal and gate to heaven or hell,
kingdom of old and new.

What do you see and become?
I need answers to the questions that keep my mind and body awake at
night.
They bother me so...

Drip Drip Drip

The top of the mountain goes tock, clock, tock
where is the spinach in hill?
It's outside playing basketball…
tickity tickity toctoc toc,
I think we can play
a bee bock hop!!!
ONE 2 Three
Under the tree I can see the bluebird's bee
to you
Always…

OCTOBER 1, 2000

Once I was afraid
I feared I could never live without me by your side,
BUT KNOW I'M Strong,
and I thank my mother.

        Only God knows how it will grow

OCTOBER 2, 2000

Balance...
the coming together of two people,
two powers...
the alliance with one another is so beautiful...
kindness...Peace... Love...Happiness...

OCTOBER 3, 2000

The Ninth Gate is so good,
I just wish there was more to it
so I could understand it better.

Now I'm curious if there is some book or place out there really like that.
It's just so interesting,
the devil, you know, and God.

I wonder about death and its place on the earth
Mystery and spiritual things are so neat and real to me
I believe they whisper in my head.

No matter how they sound,
I wish I could learn more and find out the things I seek
adventure calls to me,
my friend and lover.

OCTOBER 4, 2000

Why do people feel the need to create drama in every situation?
It's sick really
that they like to gossip and talk dirt about others
without that key person knowing it.

That certain someone must feel really shitty after all is said and done.
I'm sorry to have ears and listen to such cruelty,
the old "see no evil, hear no evil, speak no evil"
is never followed,
never learned or spoken of
now it's just the opposite in society's teaching—
sickening really.

Who is true,
who is really to be loved and cherished?
My head is always in the line of fire,
even when I don't put it there, why?
Survival of the fittest, not the nicest, I guess.

OCTOBER 5, 2000

Hey Buddie!!! 'Sup???
How are you,
how's your day,
how's your life been, family, boy/girlfriend?

I don't know,
sometimes I like to talk about other people's feelings and lives
besides my own
now I don't feel so vain...
you know?

October 7, 2000

Please don't spoil my day.

Why do we run???
From the things that
scare us?

To you who are so great!
I do not see you,
I do not hear from you...

Do you believe in me???
So I ask,
in yourself???

Yes, I shall ask
one small question:
who am I?

How do I realize
my intention?
The answer comes
from within...

Do you believe in me?
In yourself?

What a bunch of selfish, ungrateful people ...

So full of conformity,
so wanting to be liked,
understood by the main character,
the one who doesn't know what's going on.

Under his clownish devil grin...
the one that lurks,
learning in the dark
the evil, selfless one.

Without the one
no one likes,
no one is nobody.

Never allowed by elders to be anyone
but with that ultrarich smug ass (donkey);
the donkey feeds on the souls and uses them up till nothing's left
on a nothing of all nothings.

The one knows
one likes
but needs for selfishness.

To you
people in need,
be true, follow it,
make a stand, break down from conformity.

OCTOBER 11, 2000

Today is a good day for utter coldness
I am cold;
the weather outside is cold.

Why?
Why must it be this way?
Why do the seasons change?

I do not belong,
I frown down my tree of life
and escape to a bottomless pit.

Oh well,
farewell to late-night things.

OCTOBER 13, 2000

Friday 13th
I'm scared to death....
final destination

OCTOBER 14 AND 15

Today sucks…
It's the very first and very last day as I know it…
WOW!!!

My free being is ever so cramped,
God, how unloved by you at times…
building windows, but hiding them through walls
where is my door???

OCTOBER 16, 2000

Let me add color and life to this lonely book
every so often it's picked up and opened
my struggle to keep it real is a tough,
lonely struggle by social order.

Class, race, social identity mean nothing to me
why should it?
Why let the stupidness bother me?

Why speak my mind among the ignorant?
What good use of time is this?
Not a good use.

For who will grow the wheat?
Not me
who is that lazy pig,
that lazy mother,
that lazy world.

Yes, so we shall push all of it away and never talk of such awful things
again.
Yes, if we push hard enough, it will just disappear—
no more of that.

It's all up to us now,
so try hard and do your best to forget
forget me and the tree I sit upon.

Please forget me and my tree
we don't deserve your attention;
push us away!!!

October 25, 2000

Today I turn 16

"Let your life lightly dance on the edge of time,
like the dew on the tip of a leaf"— Rabindranath Tagore

Yes, man!!!
Me be 16!!!
Oh yeah…I'm gonna finally start my freedom!!!
I'm just calm, peaceful, and collected.
I'm gonna party!!!
Oh yeah!!!

My supposedly last day here—
I wonder what will happen and what will become of me
I am not so anxious to find out
its not like I can change the future of anything
my decision stands, so what if I know.

LOSE YOURSELF AND THE OTHERS AROUND YOU!!!

I have tossed this date over and over in my mind, and for the life of me, I do not know what Gabie's last day was to be.

In 1998 she went to live with one of my sisters (Beth) for about three months, and then in 2001 Gabie day stayed in a children's home for a few months. The home is a large estate that took children in with control or behavioral issues. Gabie was skipping school, sneaking out at night, and had become so defiant at times that our arguments would escalate to frightening heights. The school helped her get through her junior year in high school, but it did not help her control her anger. I fought for years to get Gabie into the school, and when I finally succeeded, the teachers informed me that it was too bad I hadn't brought her sooner; maybe then they could have had a chance to help her. She seemed to slip through so many cracks.

OCTOBER 31, 2000

Will it ever find me,
discover who I am,
what I stand for?

I've been waiting for so long
and still I wait...
for what?

Now it never comes,
it never appears to me
to my being
why?
Why me, why can't I find it?

I'm complete with or without it,
but yet I long for it,
for love...
All I need is love?

Mission to Mars

I saw that movie Mission to Mars
I remember a long time ago
my brother and I talked of solar seeding
as I watched that movie, our ideas came to life.
It's not fiction but true,
the movie is true!!!
WOW!!!

November 1, 2000

I wish I could make everyone listen to Bob Marley,
take away everything and make everyone feel high.
If people only got down to the roots,
the roots of the situation
it would make it that much better,
more bearable.
I feel in today's society everything on the TV, radio, and
newspapers, everything in our culture brainwashes you!!
Especially all those TV sitcoms—brainwashers!!!
Teachers' brainwashers, every politician
and news media person.
Take the artificial society—
even music, new stuff,
clothes, everything—nothing's pure, and it has subliminal messages,
we don't need money.
Just listen to old untouched words and thoughts of wisdom,
not brainwashers
everyone is depressed and unkind 'cause of things they put into their bodies,
like all the processed and chemical foods, etc.

November 6, 2000

AHHHH!!!! I went to the Jerry Garcia Band (JGB) show on Saturday, with April, Jessica, and Greta. It was so great. I danced so much, I could feel the beat of the music in my body, and I moved my body to it. It was so Great!

I got in for free too because we went there early to get tickets and the owner thought we looked good, so he put us down on the guest list. Hell yeah!! I danced so much with so many different people and just chilled It was great!! I love hippie shows.

OH HAPPY DAY!

Let the music touch your soul,
become one with the pounding beats,
feel it in your heart,
watch your body move
it's beautiful!
Oh Happy Day!

Oh Happy Day!
WOW!! Become one with your soul,
one with your mind,
feel the groove-on things
Oh Happy Day

Dance,
shake,
groove,
love your body and soul!

You are your own person,
the beauty inside you shines for everyone
Let it out!
Be free!
Oh Happy Day!

EARTH ANGEL

November 11, 2000

Today's the day,
tonight's the night
when I fall for you.

When it all comes together
but, who are you? I ask
this voice, questions in my head:
who are you???

I don't know,
but you are great
in my eyes!

I love you for all that you are
and all those nights you thought of me…thank you,
could you touch my life?

The words that touch me
speak so little
what have I done,
who have I lost?
You…
Who are you?
Speak to me,
please
No gibberish

YOU CAN SPEAK FREELY

DECEMBER 3, 2000

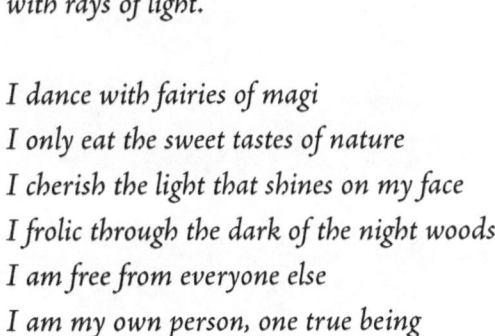

GABRIELLE

I am free
I run in my own direction
I live in the shelter of the trees
I pray to the Gods of time
I dream of the present
that whispers in my soft ears
I love the one that shines my soul
with rays of light.

I dance with fairies of magi
I only eat the sweet tastes of nature
I cherish the light that shines on my face
I frolic through the dark of the night woods
I am free from everyone else
I am my own person, one true being
I am yours for the taking.

SOMEDAY YOU WILL SEE ME

December 8, 2000

I have had enough of people's crap.
I don't need it;
they get on my damn nerves.

My loving soul has diminished to nothing
who, what have I BECOME?
My flower-power life is gone
it's now corrupted by the people who can't break free.

My soul is free—
it will always be—
but my mind is in reality
I must get away from it all.

It bothers me too much
I want to be set free
like the Indians, on my own natural path.

God and nature are the eyes and my world
I cherish you and your beauty
watch over me and show me love....

December 13, 2000

Who is the person I see before me?
Who is she?
Does she really exist?

A real person,
real feelings,
in a deep hearted.

WHAT A STUPID, STUPID GIRL!!!

What do you know?
What good are you to me?
*I don't give a **** about you!*
You're the one I keep around
for laughs and shakes
on those hours of boredom
when I've got nothing better to do but leer my golden eyes on you...

You're nothing to me,
the shit on my boots
I own your body and soul.
I love shoving you around
you make it so easy
you're weak,
only good for pleasure of the senses.

I'm Insecure.

I don't believe in you,
I'm selfish

I don't trust you,
I'm insecure.

I don't need you,
I'm dumb!!!

I can do better than you,
I don't comprehend well!

I like to ****,
I love you…

Let's all be sick, nasty people,
whips to your mates,

**** toys,
love ships,

a prize,
a trophy, a bitch, a sweetheart.

With the stars of tomorrow…

With the stars of tomorrow I will believe in you, in your kind,
in your past on the life I only knew but once,
in the truth of your eyes

I love you;
you're a beauty in my eyes.
I look up to you,
see you for the realness you are.

You can only feel me in the physical of the night,
in the mystical night,
flowers of gods, nature's own
love, palms of life and death.

The truth I see with my very own eye
is the way my own eyes work and feel your touch,
oh-be soft to touch.

Of a berry blooming on the small tree of life and death,
the death of a friend can kill you
the death of a loved one will charm you into believing you're a chimp
of great importance,
the kind of importance one needs to share in a
world of destruction and life.

I'm Vain

You say I'm a stupid person,
and I'm vain, and you're probably right.

Tell me, show me
how can I show you I love and care for you?

Please quit hanging up on me
and forgetting my feelings,
who I am and how I take things.

Vain, that's me vain
I guess so, I'm vain as shit.
I know who I am,
how I look and feel.

Let me focus on you
that's what you want, right?
You don't see me in the right light.

Vain,
that's Me, I am, I'm vain,
I admit it.

I must get out of self-love and pity,
I must
for your sake.

Dream of me tonight

Love me, tell me what to do
I need you for this.

Choose my day and the sign of it
naked we lay laughing at ourselves
how it must be.

Don't Anger Me!

December 26, 2000

I count the hours till I can talk to you,
see you, hold you tight in my weak arms
I dream of you.

I've got a feeling in my stomach and chest,
maybe anxiety, maybe not, maybe it's you
I do believe you've touched my life, my heart.

I love you and your touch
the softness sends shivers all over me
when I'm with you, butterflies enter me, and my focused world becomes on
you.

Please give me a second chance,
let me love you
I long to be near you and touch you softly.

I love you.

January 14, 2001

I hate my given soul mate,
the given one from the depths of my hell;

my purpose on earth
to feel the need to become part of an emotional attachment.

**** it...
**** these urges I have to take care of you,
to reach hold of your arm.

Forget these feelings I have for you
tuck them into a small box,
push it under your bed
or in a closet.

**** this life I share with a insult,
forget his beauty
and truth...

Forget the sacred name of a past,
forget the past
forget about me too.

January 19, 2001

Sometimes I just feel like putting my head down and crying
forgetting it all would be bliss.
Too much stress and agony in me.
I hurt people, and they do it right back of course, unintentionally.

But I can't get my thoughts straight and clear,
I feel like I'm missing something
no longer happy, Why?

I should start to grieve over an asshole
instead I choose not to, but continue with him—why?
I don't know how to make up my mind on the situation.

I know I should drop him like a bad habit,
but habits are so hard to break
I just set myself up to be pathetic
I'm really not
I know that

I wish he did; he won't though
I'm probably just some girl he thinks he can get with any time,
but I'm not.
I just don't care anymore.

So why try?
There's no reason to, so I don't
I'll just cheat on his dumb ass
no, I won't; I know I won't, maybe?

Who knows, I could if I really wanted to
I mean I won't feel bad,
I'm sure he doesn't feel bad for the shit he's done.

Two pints of booze!
Tell me…
Ace you a bad fish too?
Everyone around me sees me as someone else

January 29, 2001

Shadows in my heart,
the words you say:
look and see for yourself
before your untimely death.

Understand this,
not that which blinds you from guilt
this is to you
who creeps in the dark.

Never knowing or showing
the wrong
evilness one has
don't look at me and tell me I'm wrong.

For sleepless nights and heart-filled hours
of guilt and sorrow,
please, see you are just as bad.

Like a wolf who only knows to hunt and prey upon weak ones,
never knowing the pain they cry out
in a silent voice
when you play with their mischievous heads.

Please believe it
when they tell you, the wolf,
you are not innocent.

Please know you don't do no wrong
in the eyes of the one who tries to please you
with sweet touches and artifacts of the world and one's self.

Try to believe in the one you gaze upon in the mirror has faults too
and can hurt a weakling
just as easily as a lover can hurt you.

Believe it when the lover of a rose
as red as the blood-stained sheets you lie your back upon
and have shared with many more,
that you too have thorns that prick on the fingers of the lover.

The one who you ask to change and come back to self-confidence,
these things you ask of your lover
are all fine and dandy
and to be expected in a desperate time of need.

But remember,
the wolf is in you and can and does prick and hurt
the hands and hearts of the mischievous lovers,
remember all wolves and roses can change
no guilt trips for me
for I'm not the only guilty one.

138

Oh Dear Lord

Oh high and mighty,
I have taken your place,
robbed you blind and stole your heart.

Please forgive me for my doings
please understand me for a glory of nature,
a pause at your mire surface.

Please hold me in the same respect as your arms come together
please allow me to cry,
to love you no more.

You're a thorn
torn from my forgiving soul.

Let my blood vein pop,
burst onto your soul.

Please, oh high and mighty lover,
great being of life and death,
allow me to enter

Please be.

Do you really love me?

Do you really have good intentions for me and my soul?
Promise me you'll be and stay true to me
can you do that;
will your heart let you?

Could you be telling the truth,
or do your eyes lie to me,
long for me?

Do you really dream about me,
wait for me?

Where do I really stand in your eyes,
would you really honor me
do anything for me?

Do you keep the scent of our love in your mind,
body and soul
do you really know me or yourself for all that matters?

Do you need me,
do you understand me
do you want me and my mind?

Will you go out of your way for me ,
when I really need you?

Will you always be there for me, or try?
Do you promise to be faithful in your heart to me?

Do you like me for all that I am,
love me for the same?
Do you respect me and my body
did you ever?

Do you really know how I feel?
Do you really know how I see you,
do you really need me,
love me? Forever?

Unknown date, seventeen years old

The tears of the bitter pain,
wherever it may be,
the chilling cold or the freezing rain gives me a little reality;
the abuse and the lies hurt me more yesterday.

The stinging pain of my saddened eyes will keep me from crying today
the coldness of my heart will end, because I have hope
the scattered pieces of my broken mind will mend, because I have learned to
cope.

It crawls upon my skin what you should think of me
I feel the stares, judgmental eyes,
watch what I say,
watch what I do, but it's not you, it's me.

My fear makes my thoughts silent,
magnifies my faults, so I fight it,
since when fear wins,
am I who you think I should be?

More afraid of not flying than of falling,
more afraid to hide away my feelings than of bawling,
more afraid to sit in silence than to speak for myself,
more afraid to sit back and watch
than to stick up for myself, someone.

More afraid to close my mind than to open my eyes and see,
more afraid to close my heart than to let in diversity,

more afraid of falling,
more afraid of not trying than of failing,
more afraid of not thinking than of letting my imagination go sailing,
more afraid to settle for less than to keep striving,
more afraid of not living than of dying

maybe when it comes, I'll be smarter,
or maybe when it comes, I'll be pretty,
maybe I'll be funnier, or be in the crowd,
or maybe the boys will like me

maybe I'll have hair like her, or act like her,
maybe I'll dress like her,
or maybe, just maybe, I'll be me,
and when it comes, I'll finally be okay with that.

Consciously I tiptoe about my life, stepping softly slowly,
careful not to make a peep,
and all it takes is that one small step
for me to fall through the floor into the arms of the person
I want to be
but I am to afraid to find.

Leaving you all,
love you've forgotten,
every soft whisper,
good night cursed,
simple smiles,
secret glances,
sweet aromas satisfied.

The memory of our past evaporated,
those soft touches lost,
fluttering heartbeats melted
sorrow no longer lives in my heart.

I know not your name,
I still love you more and more
the more I am around, the more I seem to be missing
I take a quick look around

the door,
hoping to see you
standing there
looking at me
with a smile,
but around the door you're not there.

I can't find you
I can't see you,
your smiling face looking at me
sometimes I like to think that you were the one to show me the way…
so if you are standing behind the door,
please show me the way…

                    In memory of my beloved WI friend
                        If you can hear me, I miss you!!!…

To my friend
who may not know it
but mean so much to me
all of you!!!

145

The Tapped Paper

Wait!
What's this?
You don't care, you say
have you ever?
I say.

Why?
Why do you demand this turmoil?
Don't you understand
you've hurt me
by the things you say and do.

Before I started out with you,
I loved my ways
then the jokester entered my life and changed my heart
on the day of the night of the devil,
in a beautiful place what is forever cold and bitter.

From then on my focused words, thoughts, and deeds became all so different,
real,
something to touch, hold on to, to love, to share,
but never once did the boy, the jokester, you, tell the paper,
the weakling, me.

You came for me or confronted me
maybe in thought or deed,

maybe in your own way
but never words.

Tonight I tell you the truth and feel sorrow in my voice
in reply the jokester laughs at the weakling and hangs up,
not knowing or caring how the paper feels in his shaky hands.

What's gonna happen next
a phone call perhaps at teatime
and a laugh from the little boy, the jokester himself, or his victim?

Why? Why choose an emotion of such beauty,
so free, so wild (love), to abuse and bruise, play with
doesn't this tear, this sigh,
the voice who puts forth the effort on you mean shit.

In your helpless, harmful eyes
do you feel bad for the crime you've committed on a weakling?
May I die tonight and you feel remorse and sorrow of it al,l having lived
your life like you're gonna be here tomorrow,
never letting loved ones in for a good look.

Why not say the things you need to
just in case you die before you wake
know somewhere in you
you did all you could to keep our memory going,
a caring kind one at that—why?

Oh dear God, please speak softly to the flat, touchable paper,
the weakling, the taken wench, tell her, me, how you feel.
Let me be myself and love you for all that you are.

147

Open your cage door and come out and play with me,
imagination is the key to life; explore your thoughts
please act like I mean something to you.

Don't treat me like that,
but you will anyways.
As for me I'll just let wounds and egos heal with time.

But the young boy, the jokester,
must remember the flat paper on the bed is fragile and can be torn easily.
Every day when light hits my eyes,
when the unspoken words enter my life, my secret will remain.

The one you don't know,
here's a hint:
only for so long can a child play with an infant's imagination
before the infant goes insane and blows up.
The boy, the jokester, can sit there and wonder, "Why does all this anger
come out from the weakling?"

Know this, the only true emotion the jokester ever bestowed upon the wench
was anger.
Never once a word or thought mentioned to the weakling of happiness,
never a pleasant real emotion the weakling could touch.
Maybe the jokester's too clouded now by paper's abilities to be good in the
sense of a physical nature appealing to one's eyes of sorts.

Never did the boy know he could reach out and touch the paper
or hold it to his heart and explore it with a new shiny pen.
But the wench will admit
the few beautiful moments in the boy's life he wrote down on the paper.

I know and still believe he remembers the first time he held the weakling in his bed
on the night of the conversation with true emotions of self-pity and sorrow
on a life's dream
and the weakling's feelings,
an autumn night in the beginning of a love story.

Now with the unhappy endings,
but who's to blame?
Me, the weakling, the one who gives away too much,
shows too many sides and feelings,
the wench of the tavern,
dressed in her black gown covered with filth from a day's work.

So who the abuser, the jokester, calls the next day to tea time,
knowing full well the weakling won't give a **** about the night the jokester
played an evil rotten joke on the wench, the weakling, the touched paper,
and then laughed in her face.

Or the day he stood her up in a bitter cold winter's day,
the day the weakling got the courage to stand up to the jokester, the boy,
and he came running back to the wench.

But the role now reverses as it always does
now when again when he calls, the weakling will say "it's all right, it's okay,"
life goes on; no, don't be sorry for my feelings
I'm sorry I have them, I'm sorry I take this shit,
I'm sorry I'm not a worthwhile person in your eyes,

I'm sorry all I am is a piece of paper you can fling around and tear up,
you can always tape it back up to get what you need
what that boy doesn't know is that a piece of tape can only hold on for so

long,
so this is the end, my only friend.
I'm so sorry I'll never get to look into your heart, soul, eyes again.

As I walk along the road,

I look, I look and see kindness,
a face of love, reach for it,
touch the love in you.

Nothing's for certain; live for the day
embrace it, love it.
let me growup

Freedom calls to me:
the not knowing, not showing, how can this be?
Wow, watch the fool.

So many voices; which one to believe?
Feel free, choose me
you're the apple of my eye…let me love you.

Why do I let you enter my head
and fill my heart with hopes and dreams?

Who would be a mermaid fair,

Singing alone
combing her hair under the sea
in a golden curl
with a comb of pearl
on a throne!

JULY 3, 2001

The first day of my singleness!!!
I'm not gonna cry, and I'm gonna party!!!

Shortly after Gabie died I was visiting with a friend, who just happens to be a wonderful poet. Out of that visit, Terri gave the following gift of Gabie to Clay and I.

Gabie
by Terri Kirby Erickson

She left her body
like a coat on a bus,
a thing that served its
purpose, but forgotten.

The weightlessness
of it! The sheer joy of
unencumbered motion!
She could see for miles,

touch the tips of stars,
taste the sun. Every
sound was music, every
word a song. And

dancing had no need
for feet, nor leaping,
when heaven opened up,
and God stood, waiting.

Gabie loved to paint her furniture; I would paint it white, and she would paint over it. This happened a few times in the course of Gabie's teen-age years. The angel picture and the following words remain on her dresser today.

As you fall through
your dark
blackened hole,
don't forget the ones you stepped on your way back down to reality.

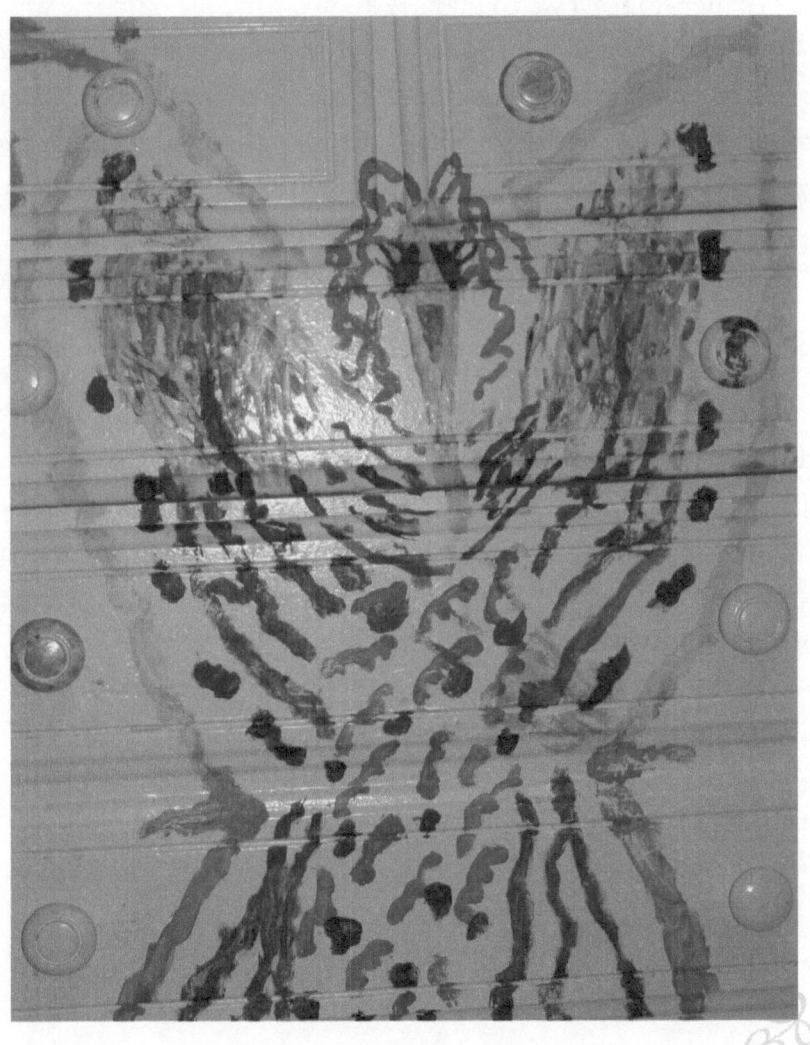

In the months following Gabie's death, I found eight of her journals in various hiding places. The above was contained in five of them. In the beginning I couldnt read her words I felt it was my task to compile them into one work. To read them was torment. In many ways this project was my way of giving her life; it has been my way of touching her.

Living with someone with anxiety and a bipolar disorder can be very trying in a roller-coaster way. But would I go back and live those days again just to be with her? Yes. Would I do things differently? Wouldn't we all change things if we could have known what the outcome was to be? I did so many things incorrectly, but I have to believe I tried to do the best I could with what I had. In my heart I will always want to hold her in my arms just one more time, but a very important thought I tell myself daily is that it was Gabie's time. No matter what I did, God was waiting for her to come to him at that very moment in her life.

Despite our struggles, we also had an abundance of our good times. Those that stand out today are the ones that we encountered close to her death.

Two weeks prior to Gabie dying and shortly after Christmas, Gabie and I went shopping. During our visit to one department store that displayed dozens of fancy hats, we laughed and giggled as we tried on the wilder ones for each other's pleasure. To this day I can hear her voice telling me how silly I was and how she loved me. It was our best shopping trip in years. During that day, I remember thinking she's growing, we're growing. We were finally starting to develop an adult relationship. I think that has been one of my hardest obstacles during this process I truly believed we were maturing, and better days were to come.

A month before Gabie died, I received my master's in library science. Gabie, Clay, and I went to the ceremony, and when my name was announced,

I heard yahoos, whistles, and a wonderful, "Yeah, Mom." At that moment I knew my daughter had a hand in the small eruption, and it brought a smile to my face. Her"Yeah, Mom" took me back to a five-year-old who stood on her chair during a similar ceremony yelling "That's My Mom," when I received an associate's degree. Later that day at the reception for new librarians, someone had taken a picture of the three of us with my camera. After I heard about Gabie's death, I remembered the film, still undeveloped. It turned out to be one of the best pictures the three of us had taken in a long time. I shall always cherish this picture and wish I could thank the individual who was kind enough to take it for us. Throughout my life, Gabie had always been one of my greatest supporters. What a wonderful child she was, is, and will always be.

Wish you were here!

Thank you,

First and foremost, I would like to thank Gabie and Clay. Without each of them, I could not be whole. Thanks to Gabie, for her words of wisdom and her gift of letting me be a part of her life for twenty-one years. Thank you to Clay, for his sense of humor and putting a smile on my face; you're a wonderful son. To my sisters, for always being there with unquestionable love. And to each and every one of my family and extended family members for keeping Gabie's memory alive and their continued support and love of each other.

And thank you to my mother, for she made me strong.

Thank you Alicia, Andrea, Austin, Beth, Chloe, Cindy, Craig, Deavon, Dennis, Duke, Ellie, Ethan, Gene, Hannah, Jane, Jillian, Jessica, Joel, Josie, Julie, Justin, Kelly, Kieran, Karlye, Mary, Maureen, Michelle, Mikayla, Melissa, Nancy, Peyton, Riley, Ross, Ryan, Sam, Scott, Steve, Steven, Tara, Terri, Travis, Vickie, and Zack.

About the Author

Gabie was born October 25th 1984 in Mt. Clemmons, Michigan.
At the age of two and a half, her family moved to Winston-Salem,
North Carolina where she resided until her death
on January 31st, 2006.